MW00628964

Who first became a child of God
and shared in his life in baptism on

....

────────────

who was nourished by the body
and blood of Jesus
for the first time on

May 16, 2004

────────────

who was given the gift of
the Holy Spirit to follow Jesus on

....

At the Last Supper, Jesus changed bread and wine into his Body and Blood. This was the first Holy Mass. Then Jesus said to his apostles, "Do this in memory of me."

New . . . Saint Joseph

CHILDREN'S MISSAL

**An Easy Way of
Participating at Mass
for Boys and Girls**

With Official Text of People's Parts
of the Holy Mass
Printed in Bold Type

CATHOLIC BOOK PUBLISHING CO.
New Jersey

Nihil Obstat: Daniel V. Flynn, J.C.D., Censor Librorum

Imprimatur: ✠ James P. Mahoney, D.D.,
Vicar General, Archdiocese of New York

The publishers wish to thank Rev. Nicholas Capetola, C.R.M.
for his great help in the publication of this book.

INDEX

Introduction   7
Holy Mass   8
    Liturgy of the Word   21
    Liturgy of the Eucharist   30
Life of Christ   65
Prayers   86

(T-806)

© 1998-1977 by Catholic Book Publishing Co.,
Printed in China

Dear Boys and Girls:

THIS is your own missal. Take it with you when you go to Mass. It will help you to please God, to adore and thank him, to praise and love him.

On almost every page of the Mass section of this book, you will find a picture and a prayer. The picture will show you what the priest is doing and the prayer will help you to pray with the priest and people. The words in heavy black type are said aloud by everyone.

At one of the important parts of the Mass every Sunday, the priest reads a Gospel that will teach you something that Jesus said and did. The section on "The life of Christ in Pictures" will help you to know our Lord's life better and to take a more active part at every Mass.

HOLY MASS

ON THE CROSS Christ offered his Body and Blood to God the Father for us. In the Mass this great act is repeated.

Mass begins with *Introductory Rites* (page 11). We speak to God in acts of contrition, praise and petition.

Then follows the *Liturgy of the Word* (page 21). We listen to what God says to us in the Readings, the Gospel and the Homily.

The *Liturgy of the Eucharist* (page 30), has three parts.

(1) With the priest we present the gifts of the bread and wine *(Preparation of the Gifts,* page 30).
(2) At the consecration this bread and wine is changed into the Body and Blood of Christ *(Eucharistic Prayer,* page 35).
(3) In Holy Communion we receive Christ who has given himself in love *(Communion Rite,* page 51).

Mass ends with the blessing and the dismissal *(Concluding Rite,* page 61).

We sing hymns to praise God and to show our joy at Mass.

OBJECTS FOR MASS

The Altar is a kind of table where the gifts of the sacrifice and the food of the banquet are prepared.

The Crucifix shows the sacrifice of Jesus which is re-presented at Mass.

The Chalice is a cup which contains the wine that will be changed into the Blood of Jesus and become our drink at this sacred meal.

The Host is bread that will be changed into the Body of Jesus and become our food at this sacred meal.

The Missal or Sacramentary is a large book from which the priest reads the prayers.

The Lectionary is a large book on a stand or Lectern, from which the Word of God is read to the people.

Candles are a symbol of our love for God.

ENTRANCE PROCESSION — Mass begins with an entrance song during which the priest and his ministers come to the altar.

THE ORDER OF MASS

INTRODUCTORY RITES

STAND

♩ ♩ ♫ **ENTRANCE SONG** ♫ ♫

All make the sign of the cross:

PRIEST: In the name of the Father, and of the Son, and of the Holy Spirit.

PEOPLE: **Amen.**

THE GREETING

One of the following forms is used:
(Shown by A, B, or C)

A

PRIEST: The grace of our Lord Jesus Christ and the love of God and the fellowship of the Holy Spirit be with you all.

PEOPLE: **And also with you.**

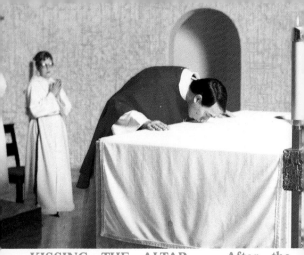

KISSING THE ALTAR — After the entrance procession, the priest shows reverence for the altar, symbol of Christ, with a kiss. Then he says the greeting.

B

OR

PRIEST: The grace and peace of God our Father and the Lord Jesus Christ be with you.

PEOPLE: Blessed be God, the Father of our Lord Jesus Christ.

OR

PEOPLE: And also with you.

C   **OR**

PRIEST: The Lord be with you.

PEOPLE: And also with you.

THE PENITENTIAL RITE

The people are invited to be sorry for their sins.

PRIEST: My brothers and sisters, to prepare ourselves to celebrate the sacred mysteries, let us call to mind our sins.

Then one of the following forms is used.

A

PRIEST and PEOPLE:

**I confess to almighty God,
and to you, my brothers and sisters,
that I have sinned through my own
    fault** They strike their breasts:

**in my thoughts and in my words,
in what I have done,
and in what I have failed to do;
and I ask blessed Mary, ever virgin,
all the angels and saints,
and you, my brothers and sisters,
to pray for me to the Lord our God.**

B   OR

PRIEST: Lord, we have sinned against you: Lord, have mercy.

PEOPLE: Lord, have mercy.

PRIEST: Lord, show us your mercy and love.

PEOPLE: And grant us your salvation.

C   OR

PRIEST or other minister:
You were sent to heal the contrite:
Lord, have mercy.

PEOPLE: Lord, have mercy.

PRIEST or other minister:
You came to call sinners:
Christ, have mercy.

PEOPLE: Christ, have mercy.

PRIEST or other minister:
You plead for us at the right hand of the Father:
Lord, have mercy.

PEOPLE: Lord, have mercy.
(Other invocations may be used)

At the end of any of the forms of the penitential rite is said:

PRIEST: May almighty God have mercy on us, forgive us our sins, and bring us to everlasting life.

PEOPLE: Amen.

THE KYRIE

Unless it is included in the penitential rite, the Kyrie is sung or said by the people with the choir or cantor.

℣. Lord, have mercy.

℟. **Lord, have mercy.**

℣. Christ, have mercy.

℟. **Christ, have mercy.**

℣. Lord, have mercy.

℟. **Lord, have mercy.**

THE GLORIA — We praise God by recalling the words sung by the angels when Jesus was born.

THE GLORIA

GLORY to God in the highest,
   and peace to his people on earth.
Lord God, heavenly King,
almighty God and Father,
   we worship you, we give you thanks,
   we praise you for your glory.
Lord Jesus Christ, only Son of the
   Father,
Lord God, Lamb of God,
you take away the sin of the world:
   have mercy on us;
you are seated at the right hand of
   the Father:
   receive our prayer.
For you alone are the Holy One,
you alone are the Lord,
you alone are the Most High,
   Jesus Christ,
   with the Holy Spirit,
   in the glory of God the Father.
   Amen.

THE OPENING PRAYER — We join with the priest silently as he prays aloud for all people.

THE OPENING PRAYER

PRIEST: Let us pray.

Priest and people pray silently for a while. Then the priest says the opening prayer, which gives the theme of the particular celebration and asks God to help us. Then he says:

We ask you this
    through our Lord Jesus Christ,
    your Son,
    who lives and reigns with you
    and the Holy Spirit,
    one God,
    for ever and ever.

PEOPLE: **Amen.**

THE FIRST READING — We listen to the reader as he proclaims God's Word.

Liturgy of  the WORD

SIT

THE FIRST READING

God Speaks to Us through the Prophets

We sit and listen to the word of God as it was spoken through his prophets and apostles. The Reader takes their place in speaking to us.

At the end of the reading:

READER: The word of the Lord.

PEOPLE: **Thanks be to God.**

RESPONSORIAL PSALM — We recite or sing a part of a psalm to show that we accept God's Word which was just read.

RESPONSORIAL PSALM

The people repeat the response sung or said by the reader the first time and then after each verse.

Then follows

THE SECOND READING

God Speaks to Us through the Apostles

At the end:

READER: The word of the Lord.

PEOPLE: Thanks be to God.

Jesus will speak to us in the gospel. We rise now out of respect and prepare for his message with the alleluia.

STAND

ALLELUIA

The people repeat the alleluia after the reader's alleluia and then after the verse.

THE GOSPEL — The priest now reads the Gospel in the name of Jesus, and Jesus himself becomes present among us through his Word.

THE GOSPEL

STAND

DEACON (or priest):

The Lord be with you.

PEOPLE: **And also with you.**

✠ A reading from the holy gospel according to N.

PEOPLE: **Glory to you, Lord.**

We listen to the priest or deacon proclaim the Word of God.

At the end the deacon (or priest) says:

The gospel of the Lord.

PEOPLE: **Praise to you, Lord Jesus Christ.**

THE HOMILY

SIT

God Speaks to Us through the Priest

The Homily helps us to put the words of Christ into practice.

PROFESSION OF FAITH — We tell God we believe all that he has taught us.

THE PROFESSION OF FAITH

WE BELIEVE in one God   **STAND**
    the Father, the Almighty,
    maker of heaven and earth,
    of all that is seen and unseen.

WE BELIEVE in one Lord, Jesus Christ,
   the only Son of God,
   eternally begotten of the Father,
   God from God, Light from Light,
   true God from true God,
   begotten, not made, one in Being
      with the Father.

Through him all things were made.
For us men and for our salvation
   he came down from heaven:

All bow at the following words up to:
and became man.

by the power of the Holy Spirit,
he was born of the Virgin Mary,
   and became man.

For our sake he was crucified under
      Pontius Pilate;
   he suffered, died, and was buried.

On the third day he rose again
      in fulfillment of the Scriptures;
he ascended into heaven
      and is seated at the right hand of
         the Father.

He will come again in glory to judge
the living and the dead,
and his kingdom will have no end.

WE BELIEVE in the Holy Spirit,
the Lord, the giver of life,
who proceeds from the Father
and the Son.

With the Father and the Son he is
worshiped and glorified.

He has spoken through the Prophets.

We believe in one holy catholic and
apostolic Church.

We acknowledge one baptism for the
forgiveness of sins.

We look for the resurrection of the
dead,
and the life of the world to come.
Amen.

*In celebrations of Masses with Children, the Apostles'
Creed, p. 87, may replace the Profession of Faith
given above.*

GENERAL INTERCESSIONS — We unite with one another to pray for the needs of our community, the whole Church, and all people.

PEOPLE: Lord, hear our prayer.
(or other response)

At the end the priest says the concluding prayer: **PEOPLE: Amen.**

Liturgy of the EUCHARIST

THE PREPARATION OF THE GIFTS

OFFERTORY SONG — While the gifts of the people are brought forward to the priest and are placed on the altar, the offertory song is sung.

Blessed are you, Lord,
God of all creation.
Through your goodness we have this
　　bread to offer,
which earth has given and human hands
　　have made.
It will become for us the bread of life.

If there is no singing, the response is:

PEOPLE: Blessed be God for ever.

PREPARATION OF THE WINE — The
priest thanks God for giving us the wine
that will be changed into Christ's blood.

Blessed are you, Lord, God of all creation.
Through your goodness we have this wine
   to offer,
fruit of the vine and work of human hands.
It will become our spiritual drink.

If there is no singing the response is:

PEOPLE: Blessed be God for ever.

INVITATION TO PRAYER

PRIEST: Pray, brethren, that our sacrifice may be acceptable to God, the almighty Father.

PEOPLE: May the Lord accept the sacrifice at your hands, for the praise and glory of his name, for our good, and the good of all his Church.

PRAYER OVER THE GIFTS

STAND

We ask God to Accept Our Gifts

At the end:

PEOPLE: Amen.

INTRODUCTORY DIALOGUE — The priest invites us to join with him in the words he addresses to the Father through Jesus.

EUCHARISTIC PRAYER

INTRODUCTORY DIALOGUE

PRIEST: The Lord be with you.

PEOPLE: And also with you.

PRIEST: Lift up your hearts.

PEOPLE: We lift them up to the Lord.

PRIEST: Let us give thanks to the Lord our God.

PEOPLE: It is right to give him thanks and praise.

THE PREFACE — The priest begins with a prayer of praise to God for the great works he has done for us in Jesus.

THE PREFACE
Our Prayer of Thanksgiving

Father, it is our duty and our salvation,
always and everywhere
to give you thanks
through your beloved Son, Jesus
Christ.
He is the Word through whom you
made the universe,
the Savior you sent to redeem us.
By the power of the Holy Spirit
he took flesh and was born of the
Virgin Mary.
For our sake he opened his arms on
the cross;
he put an end to death
and revealed the resurrection.
In this he fulfilled your will
and won for you a holy people.
And so we join the angels and the
saints
in proclaiming your glory
as we sing (say):

THE "HOLY, HOLY, HOLY"

First Acclamation of the People

PRIEST and PEOPLE:

Holy, holy, holy Lord, God of power
and might,

heaven and earth are full of your glory.

Hosanna in the highest.

Blessed is he who comes in the name
of the Lord.

Hosanna in the highest.

KNEEL

THE "HOLY, HOLY, HOLY" — We join with the priest and the angels to praise God the Father and Jesus whom he has sent.

Lord, you are holy indeed,
the fountain of all holiness.

Let your Spirit come upon these gifts
to make them holy,
so that they may become for us
the body ✠ and blood of our Lord,
Jesus Christ.

Before he was given up to death,
a death he freely accepted,
he took bread and gave you thanks.

He broke the bread,
gave it to his disciples, and said:

Take this, all of you, and eat it:

this is my body which will be given

up for you.

ELEVATION OF THE HOST — The priest shows the consecrated host to the people, places it on the paten, and genuflects in adoration.

When supper was ended, he took the cup.

Again he gave you thanks and praise, gave the cup to his disciples, and said:

Take this, all of you, and drink from it:

this is the cup of my blood,

the blood of the new and everlasting

covenant.

It will be shed for you and for all men

so that sins may be forgiven.

Do this in memory of me.

ELEVATION OF THE CHALICE — The priest shows the chalice to the people, places it on the corporal, and genuflects in adoration.

PRIEST: Let us proclaim the mystery of faith.

PEOPLE:

Christ has died,
Christ is risen,
Christ will come again.

B   OR

Dying you destroyed our death,
rising you restored our life.
Lord Jesus, come in glory.

C   OR

When we eat this bread and drink this cup,
we proclaim your death, Lord Jesus,
until you come in glory.

D   OR

Lord, by your cross and resurrection
you have set us free.
You are the Savior of the world.

In memory of his death and resurrection,

we offer you, Father, this life-giving bread,

this saving cup.

We thank you for counting us worthy

to stand in your presence and serve you.

May all of us who share in the body and blood of Christ

be brought together in unity by the Holy Spirit.

THE INTERCESSIONS — The priest prays for all the members of the Church—those who are still alive and those who have died.

Lord, remember your Church
   throughout the world;
make us grow in love
together with N. our Pope,
N. our bishop, and all the clergy.

For the Dead

Remember our brothers and sisters
who have gone to their rest
in the hope of rising again;
bring them and all the departed
into the light of your presence.

In Communion with the Saints

Have mercy on us all;
make us worthy to share eternal life
with Mary, the Virgin Mother of God,
with the apostles,
and with all the saints who have done
    your will throughout the ages.

May we praise you in union with them,
and give you glory
through your Son, Jesus Christ.

Concluding Doxology

Through him,
with him,
in him,
in the unity of the Holy Spirit,
all glory and honor is yours,
almighty Father,
for ever and ever.

All reply: **Amen.**

END OF EUCHARISTIC PRAYER —
Lifting up the Host and Chalice, the priest
gives glory to God through Jesus. We
join him with the word AMEN.

THE LORD'S PRAYER — Our preparation for a very close union with Jesus in Holy Communion begins with the "Our Father," the prayer which Jesus taught us to say.

THE LORD'S PRAYER

PRIEST: Let us pray with confidence to the Father in the words our Savior gave us.

STAND

PRIEST and PEOPLE:
Our Father, who art in heaven,
   hallowed be thy name;
   thy kingdom come;
   thy will be done on earth as it is in
      heaven.

Give us this day our daily bread;
and forgive us our trespasses
as we forgive those who trespass
      against us;
and lead us not into temptation,
but deliver us from evil.

PRIEST: Deliver us, Lord, from every evil, and grant us peace in our day.

In your mercy keep us free from sin
and protect us from all anxiety
as we wait in joyful hope
for the coming of our Savior,
Jesus Christ.

PEOPLE: **For the kingdom, the power
and the glory are yours, now and
for ever.**

SIGN OF PEACE

*The priest says the prayer for peace and
concludes:*

PRIEST: For ever and ever.

PEOPLE: **Amen.**

PRIEST: The peace of the Lord be with
you always.

PEOPLE: **And also with you.**

SIGN OF PEACE — Now we exchange a sign of peace and love, according to local custom.

PRIEST: Let us offer each other the sign of peace.

BREAKING OF THE BREAD — The priest breaks the bread showing that we must all share of the one Body who is Christ.

BREAKING OF THE BREAD

The people sing or say:

Lamb of God, you take away the sins
of the world:

have mercy on us.

Lamb of God, you take away the sins
of the world:

have mercy on us.

Lamb of God, you take away the sins
of the world:

grant us peace.

PRAYERS BEFORE COMMUNION —
The priest invites us to receive Jesus our
Savior who comes to us in Communion.

PRIEST: This is the Lamb of God who
takes away the sins of the world.
Happy are those who are called to his
supper.

COMMUNION OF THE PRIEST — The priest prays with us, asking God to make us worthy to receive him.

PRIEST and PEOPLE :

Lord, I am not worthy to receive you, but only say the word and I shall be healed.

He then receives Communion.

COMMUNION of the PEOPLE
—As the priest shows us the Host, we express our faith that we are receiving Jesus the Lord.

PRIEST: The body of Christ.

PEOPLE: Amen.

♫ COMMUNION SONG ♫

The Communion Song is sung while communion is given to the faithful.

SIT

SILENCE AFTER COMMUNION

After communion there may be a period of silence, or a song of praise may be sung.

PRAYER AFTER COMMUNION

STAND

PRIEST: Let us pray.

Priest and people may pray silently for a while. Then the priest says the prayer after Communion.

At the end:

PRIEST: Through Christ our Lord.

PEOPLE: Amen.

THE BLESSING — Before ending the Celebration, the priest gives us God's blessing.

CONCLUDING RITE

We have heard God's Word and eaten the body
of Christ. Now it is time for us to leave, to do
good works, to praise and bless the Lord in our
daily lives.

*After any brief announcements (sit), the
blessing and dismissal follow:*

THE BLESSING

STAND

PRIEST: The Lord be with you.

PEOPLE: And also with you.

PRIEST: May almighty God bless you,
the Father,
and the Son,
✠ and the Holy Spirit.

PEOPLE: Amen.

DISMISSAL

DEACON (or priest):

A Go in the peace of Christ.

B The Mass is ended, go in peace.

C Go in peace to love and serve the Lord.

PEOPLE: Thanks be to God.

Let us Sing Joyfully to the Lord.

RECESSIONAL — The priest dismisses us
and we go home to live as good Christians.

JESUS CHRIST
Our Lord and Savior

The
LIFE OF CHRIST
IN PICTURES

✠

Each Sunday and feastday Mass contains parts that change in accord with the particular mystery of Christ's life. In this way, the prayers at Mass recall for us the Life, Death, Resurrection and Ascension of Jesus.

This section will help you to know our Lord's life better, so you can take a more active part at every Mass during the year.

THE ANNUNCIATION—The angel Gabriel is sent from God to the Virgin Mary to tell her that she will bear a Son, Jesus. He will be the Son of God and save all people.

THE VISITATION—Mary visits her cousin Elizabeth. Elizabeth praises Mary's great faith and calls her "blessed among women."

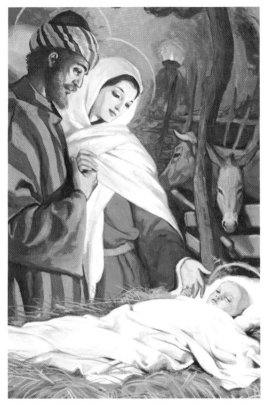

JESUS IS BORN—Jesus is born in a stable because there is no room for him and his Mother Mary and Joseph at the local inn.

THE NAME JESUS—Eight days after his birth, Mary's Son is named Jesus. This name means that he came to save us from our sins and bring us to heaven.

JESUS IN THE TEMPLE—At the age of twelve Jesus becomes separated from his parents for three days. They find him in the temple with the teachers.

JESUS IS TEMPTED—In the desert, the devil tries to have Jesus do something wrong. Jesus refuses and drives the Evil One away.

JESUS CHANGES WATER INTO WINE— When the wine runs out at a marriage feast, Mary asks Jesus to help. He has six jars filled with water. When the head waiter tastes it, it has become wine.

JESUS CLEANSES THE TEMPLE—Jesus finds merchants and money-changers in the Temple, his Father's house. He drives them out, saying: "My house is a house of prayer."

JESUS WANTS GOOD DEEDS—Jesus tells his disciples that a good tree bears good fruit. In the same way, good people do good deeds.

JESUS ESCAPES DEATH—Jesus tells the people that God is displeased by their sins. Some of them become angry and try to stone him, but he passes right through them.

JESUS SPEAKS FROM A BOAT—So many people come to hear Jesus speak that they almost crush him. He gets into a boat and continues speaking about God to them.

JESUS URGES KINDNESS — Jesus wants us to be kind to everyone. If we hurt anyone, we must tell him we are sorry. Then God will be pleased and hear our prayers.

THE MIRACULOUS CATCH OF FISH — One day Jesus tells Peter to row to the middle of the lake to fish. Peter obeys although he had fished all night and caught nothing. He catches so many fish that his boat almost sinks.

JESUS CURES A PARALYTIC — Some men bring a paralyzed man to Jesus. Because of their faith, Jesus forgives the man his sins and then cures him completely.

JESUS AND THE ROMAN OFFICER — A Roman Officer has faith that Jesus can cure his sick servant boy even from a distance. Jesus praises the man's faith and cures his servant.

JESUS RAISES A WIDOW'S SON — Jesus meets a funeral procession for the only son of a widow. He feels sorry for the mother and brings her son back to life.

JESUS TELLS US GOD IS GOOD — Jesus tells his disciples how God feeds the birds and how beautiful he makes lilies. He shows that God will take care of us too.

JESUS CURES A BLIND MAN — A blind
man hears that Jesus is passing by and
cries out to be helped. Jesus stops and
gives him sight because of his faith.

JESUS SPEAKS OF THE FATHER — Jesus
tells his disciples about God the Father. He
wants all people to know that the Father
is powerful and good.

MIRACLE OF THE LOAVES—Those who have come to hear Jesus are hungry and have no food. Jesus blesses five loaves and two fish, and feeds over 5,000 people.

JESUS CALMS THE STORM—Jesus is in a boat which is in danger of sinking because of a storm. He tells the winds to be still, and there is a great calm.

TRUE HAPPINESS—Jesus talks to the people about true happiness. We must be poor in spirit and at peace with one another. Above all, we must love God.

JESUS APPEARS IN GLORY—Peter, James, and John see Jesus in glory with Moses and Elijah. They hear a voice from heaven saying: "This is my beloved Son; hear him."

JESUS CURES A DEAF-MUTE—A man who cannot hear or speak comes to Jesus. Jesus puts his fingers in his ears, touches his tongue and says: "Be opened." The man is cured.

PRAISE OF MARY—A woman praises Jesus' Mother. Jesus remembers how Mary always obeyed God. He says that all who obey God as she did are to be praised.

JESUS CURES A SICK BOY—A royal official begs Jesus to come and cure his sick son. Jesus says: "Go home: your son lives." At that moment the boy is cured.

JESUS RAISES A DEAD GIRL—The young daughter of Jairus is dead. Jesus goes to her, takes her hand, and says: "Little girl, get up." She rises and begins to walk around.

JESUS CURES TEN LEPERS—Jesus cures ten lepers by sending them to the priest. Only one comes back to give him thanks. We should always thank Jesus for his goodness to us.

JESUS' DEATH AND RESURRECTION— Jesus tells his disciples that he will suffer, be put to death, and rise on the third day. He will go through all this to save all peopie.

THE PEOPLE PRAISE JESUS—Jesus rides into Jerusalem on a donkey. The people wave palm branches and shout: "Blessed is he who comes in the name of the Lord."

JESUS TELLS US TO OBEY JUST LAWS— Jesus is shown a coin of a government. He says we must give governments what belongs to them (like just taxes) and give God what belongs to God (like our whole self).

THE LAST SUPPER—The night before his death, Jesus changes bread and wine into his Body and Blood. He tells the disciples to do the same thing in remembrance of him.

THE SPIRIT OF JESUS—Jesus tells his disciples he is returning to the Father who sent him. He will send them the Holy Spirit to take his place and help them always.

JESUS IS SENTENCED TO DEATH—Jesus is brought before the Roman governor and sentenced to death even though he has done no wrong. He accepts his sentence in order to save us.

DEATH OF JESUS—After being beaten, Jesus is nailed to a cross. His Mother and John the disciple stand by him. After three hours of terrible pain, he dies and wins salvation for all.

RESURRECTION OF JESUS—On the third day after his death, Jesus rises again and enters into his glory. We too will rise with him to glory provided we follow him by our lives.

APPEARANCE OF THE RISEN JESUS—
Jesus appears to the apostles but Thomas
is absent and refuses to believe. Jesus
returns and tells Thomas to touch him.
Thomas says: "My Lord and my God."

ASCENSION OF JESUS—Jesus spends
forty days with his disciples after his resurrection teaching them many things. Then
he returns to his Father to await them in
heaven

PRAYERS

The Our Father

See page 51.

The Hail Mary

HAIL Mary, full of grace! the Lord is with thee; blessed art thou among women, and blessed is the fruit of thy womb, Jesus. Holy Mary, Mother of God, pray for us sinners, now and at the hour of our death. Amen.

The Glory Be

GLORY be to the Father, and to the Son, and to the Holy Spirit. As it was in the beginning, is now, and ever shall be, world without end. Amen.

The Apostles' Creed

I believe in God, the Father almighty,
    creator of heaven and earth.
I believe in Jesus Christ, his only Son, our
        Lord.
    He was conceived by the power of the
        Holy Spirit
    and born of the Virgin Mary.
    He suffered under Pontius Pilate,
        was crucified, died, and was buried.
    He descended to the dead.
    On the third day he rose again.
    He ascended into heaven,
        and is seated at the right hand of the
        Father.
        He will come again to judge the living
        and the dead.
I believe in the Holy Spirit,
    the holy catholic Church,
    the communion of saints,
    the forgiveness of sins,
    the resurrection of the body,
    and the life everlasting. Amen.

Act of Contrition

O MY God, I am heartily sorry for having offended you and I detest all my sins, because of your punishments, but most of all because they offend you, my God, who are all-good and deserving of all my love.

I firmly resolve, with the help of your grace, to sin no more and to avoid the near occasions of sin. Amen.

Grace before Meals

BLESS us, O Lord, and these your gifts, which we are about to receive from your bounty, through Christ our Lord. Amen.

Grace after Meals

WE THANK you, O Lord, for these gifts and for all the gifts we have received from your goodness, through Christ our Lord. Amen.

Morning Prayers

O MY God, I believe in you, I hope in you. I love you above all things. I thank you for having brought me safely through this night.

I give my whole self to you. Everything I do today, I will do to please you. Keep me, dear Jesus, from all evil. Bless my father and mother, and all those I love.

Evening Prayers

O GOD, I thank you for the many blessings I have received today. Forgive me all my sins. I am sorry for them all because I have displeased you. Bless me while I sleep so that I may do better tomorrow. Bless my father and mother and all those I love, and make them happy.

Jesus, Mary and Joseph, help me, especially in the hour of my death. Amen.

Our Father. Hail Mary.

Hail, Holy Queen

HAIL, holy Queen, Mother of mercy; hail our life, our sweetness and our hope. To you do we cry, poor banished children of Eve. To you do we send up our sighs, mourning and weeping in this valley of tears. Turn then, most gracious Advocate, your eyes of mercy toward us. And after this our exile show unto us the blessed fruit of your womb, Jesus. O clement, O loving, O sweet Virgin Mary.

The "Memorare"

REMEMBER, O most gracious Virgin Mary, that never was it known that anyone who fled to your protection, implored your help or sought your intercession, was left unaided. Inspired with this confidence, I fly to you, O Virgin of virgins, my Mother; to you do I come, before you I stand, sinful and sorrowful. O Mother of the Word Incarnate, despise not my petitions, but in your mercy hear and answer me. Amen.

THE HOLY ROSARY

THE Rosary calls to mind the most important events in the lives of Jesus and Mary. These events are called Mysteries and are divided into the following 3 groups:

The JOYFUL MYSTERIES help us to think of Mary's joy when Jesus came into the world.

The SORROWFUL MYSTERIES help us to think of Mary's great sorrow when Jesus suffered for our salvation.

The GLORIOUS MYSTERIES help us to think of the glorious Resurrection of Jesus and the Crowning of Mary as Queen of Heaven.

HOW TO SAY THE ROSARY

1. Say the Apostles' Creed.
2. Say 1 Our Father.
3. Say 3 Hail Marys.
4. Say 1 Glory Be, then announce the 1st Mystery and say 1 Our Father.
5. Say 10 Hail Marys and 1 Glory Be.
6. Announce 2nd Mystery and continue in the same way until each of the 5 Mysteries is said.

1. The Annunciation to Mary
Mary, Jesus will be your Son. Teach me to love Him.

The Five Joyful Mysteries

2. The Visitation
Mary, you visit your cousin Elizabeth. Help me to be kind.

4. The Presentation
Jesus, You are offered to God in the temple. Help me to obey.

3. The Birth of Jesus
Jesus, You are born in a stable. May I value grace above money.

5. The Finding in the Temple
Jesus, You are found with the teachers. Give me true wisdom.

The Five Sorrowful Mysteries

3. The Crowning with Thorns
Jesus, You receive a crown of thorns. Give me true courage.

1. The Agony in the Garden
Jesus, You are saddened by my sins. Give me true sorrow.

4. The Carrying of the Cross
Jesus, You carry the Cross gladly. Help me to be patient.

2. The Scourging at the Pillar
Jesus, You are whipped by the soldiers. Help me to be pure.

5. The Crucifixion
Jesus, You die on the Cross for me. Keep me in Your grace.

1. The Resurrection
Jesus, You rise from Your tomb. Help me to believe in You.

The Five

Glorious

Mysteries

2. The Ascension
Jesus, You go to Your Father in Heaven. Help me to hope in You.

4. The Assumption of Mary
Mary, You are taken to heaven. Let me be devoted to you.

3. Descent of the Holy Spirit
Holy Spirit, You come to bring grace. Help me to love God.

5. The Crowning of Mary
Mary, You are crowned Queen of Heaven. Let me serve you.

94